Jagadish Chandra Bose

THE FIRST MODERN SCIENTIST

Published in 2002 by

Rupa & Co

7/16, Ansari Road, Daryaganj
New Delhi 110 002

Offices at:
15 Bankim Chatterjee Street, Kolkata 700 073
135 South Malaka, Allahabad 211 001
PG Solanki Path, Lamington Road, Mumbai 400 007
36, Kutty Street, Nungambakkam, Chennai 600 034
Surya Shree, B-6, New 66, Shankara Park,
Basavangudi, Bangalore 560 004
3-5-612, Himayat Nagar, Hyderabad 500 029

ISBN 81-7167-681-2

Picture courtesy: The Bose Institute, Kolkata & Mona Chowdhury

Cover & Book Design by
Arrt Creations
45 Nehru Apts, Kalkaji New Delhi 110 019

Printed in India by
Gopsons Papers Ltd.
A-14, Sector- 60
Noida 201 301

Jagadish Chandra Bose

THE FIRST MODERN SCIENTIST

Dilip M. Salwi

Rupa & Co

CONTENTS

*Dedicated to
a librarian and well-wisher
Ms. Raj Kumari Chibber
for her ever helpful nature.*

CHAPTER ONE

Wireless Telegraphy

It was 1895. A large crowd of patriotic Indians gathered at the British style building of the Town Hall in Kolkata. The crowd was curious and restive. It could not make out what exactly they were about to see. These men and women were about to witness a strange and historic event. One of their own countrymen was about to demonstrate something rather unusual in the building to the Lieutenant Governor, Sir William Mackenzie, a representative, of the British Empire.

Only a handful of people in the audience and a few local press reporters knew that the demonstration was about a scientific experiment of great importance. But few realised how important the experiment was. Today, the experiment is hailed as one of the historic landmarks in the development of radio waves as a tool for communication. It was the world's first wireless communication link. It established the Indian scientist as one of the pioneers of wireless telegraphy—the technology of 'sending messages via radio signals without wires'.

The crowd stirred and everybody stood to attention as a horse-driven buggy approached the Town Hall. Soon, the Lieutenant Governor, a burly fellow alighted the buggy. He was received at the porch by a bright, young Indian with curly hair and bushy moustaches and brought him to the room where the demonstration was to take place. The British officials who had arrived with the Lieutenant Governor and the enthusiastic crowd followed the two to the room.

On a huge table was kept a series of big batteries, a curious looking big box called 'radiator' with some attachments and a switch—all connected through a pair of multi-coloured wires. Before the demonstration, the Indian inventor showed the different parts of the apparatus and explained their functions to the officials and the Lieutenant Governor.

As soon as the switch was put 'on', the Indian inventor explained, the electrical circuit got completed and the batteries high voltage electric power to the big box. The box generated a strong pulse of radio waves which the attachments 'directed' at the facing brick wall of the room.

The young Indian took the Lieutenant Governor and the officials to the rooms behind the brick wall. The next two rooms were closed. The third was empty except that it contained a small cannon, a pistol and a heap of packed gunpowder. All were connected via mechanical gadgets and a pair of wires to a device called 'coherer' which was the Indian's own invention. It was supposed to catch the radio waves and set off the cannon, pistol and gunpowder simultaneously.

After the Lieutenant Governor and officials assured themselves that no wire connection existed between the scientist's apparatus and the cannon, pistol and gunpowder and that they were separated by the two closed rooms, the Indian inventor invited the Lieutenant Governor to put the switch 'on' with his own hand.

Jagadish Chandra Bose.

The instant the Lieutenant Governor put the switch 'on', a loud bang was heard. When the officials rushed to the third room, to their amazement they found that the cannon and the pistol had fired and the gunpowder had exploded, sending a cloud of smoke all over the place. The demonstration was successful.

"Congratulations!" exclaimed the Lieutenant Governor, shaking the Indian's hand. "You've done the impossible! You've successfully demonstrated that it is possible to trigger off things at a distance by means of Hertzian (now called radio) waves! Commendable achievement!" The officials followed his suit and congratulated the Indian one after another.

At that historic moment, the enthusiastic and puzzled crowd realised that something impossible had been demonstrated by their countryman, something which had the nod of approval of the British rulers. Only a few however realised that the Indian inventor—a Professor at the prestigious Presidency College of Kolkata — had actually demonstrated one of the greatest modern inventions of the mankind. The wireless telegraphy or radio.

Jagadish Chandra Bose was the name of that Indian inventor.

CHAPTER TWO

The Learning Years

Jagadish Chandra Bose was born at Mymensingh, then in East Bengal (now in Bangladesh) on November 30, 1858, just a year after the India's First War of Independence was fought. His invention was also the first step towards independence in science in India. In fact, he is the first modern scientist of India.

His father, Bhagwan Chandra Bose, was a courageous and enterprising officer in the British Raj. His deeds of courage and valour were widely known in the region. He often fought with dacoits. Once he even single-handedly caught a dacoit. He was also keen to improve the living conditions of rural people. He always thought of new schemes for their benefit. Jagadish was brought up in an environment of courage, commitment and love for his country and countrymen.

Unlike the children of other officers, young Bose was specially sent to the local *pathshala* (school) in Faridpur (now in Bangladesh). His father was keen that his son should have a first-hand idea about his countrymen, their lives, dreams and aspirations. An ardent follower of the Brahmo Samaj, he wanted his son to be free from class or caste prejudices.

In the school young Jagadish's classmates were the children of the local farm labourers, farmers, fishermen and petty shopkeepers. One of them was even the son of his own domestic servant! In their company he played, roamed and dined. And he learnt a very important lesson. The love for equality, justice, fair play and brotherhood. Inspired by their stories about fields, trees, mountains and rivers, Jagadish became a nature lover and many of his later writings bear testimony to this.

Bose's father also encouraged him to become a scholar and not an officer like himself. He believed it was "better to conquer the self

than to lord over others". Often, he would take his young son for evening strolls in the neighbouring jungle and acquaint him with nature and universe around him. He would provoke the young Bose to ask a question. On occasions when he himself could not answer it he would suggest the boy that he should find out the answer himself when he grew up.

J C Bose as a young man.

It was these years spent studying nature and learning to be curious about the universe that would lead. Jagadish Chandra Bose to the path of a scholar and a scientist. It also developed the adventurous spirit that would present the world with a new vision through his wonderful inventions and discoveries.

When Bose's father was transferred to Burdwan (now West Bengal) in 1869, Jagadish was sent to St. Xavier's School in Kolkata. He was admitted to the school hostel, where he had the first taste of courage and independence. Being a villager, he soon became the butt of jokes by his classmates who were city-bred, Europeans and Anglo-Indians. They teased him, cracked jokes at his expense, and tried to overawe him. But, when on the very first day, young

Bosu Bijyam Mandir—
the house where
J C Bose used to live
and work in Kolkata.

13

Bose single-handedly fought and defeated the champion boxer of the class, everybody began to respect him. Strength wins respect and he had successfully passed the first test of independence and courage. Throughout his life Bose showed such fighting qualities in the face of heavy odds.

At Burdwan, where Bose's father became Assistant Commissioner, he set up a Technical Training School in the compound of his own bungalow. He was keen that the local rural youth should acquire technical skills and use them in setting up industries and businesses. His patriotic zeal knew no bounds. He even spent money from his own pocket to run the school!

The school had a machine shop and a foundry. Here young Bose, hardly eleven, had a first-hand exposure to machines and technicians. During vacations when he would visit Burdwan he would attend the school and learn the basic skills of carpentry, grinding, welding, moulding, etc. These skills came in handy later in designing and building sensitive instruments that made him famous across the world.

At the age of sixteen Bose joined St. Xavier's College, Kolkata, for graduate studies. Here his interest in physics was awakened by Father Lafont, a Christian missionary and astronomer, who always used novel methods of teaching science through experiments and questions.

Bose was keen to become a physician. In those pre-Independence days, when the British were ruling India, one had to go to England to study medicine. It was not likely to be easy for Bose as in the meanwhile his father had lost a fortune in his

Father Lafont

Christ's College Cambridge, 1880s.

15

enterprises for rural people and had no money left to send him abroad for higher studies.

When no other source of money came in sight, Bose's mother sold off her own jewellery and sent him to England in 1880 to study medicine. However, he could not continue his studies as the foul air in the dissecting rooms adversely affected his health.

Bose had then no option but to return India. But, then, he decided to talce up physics since it did not require dissecting bodies. Besides, physics had always fascinated him. In 1881, he therefore shifted to science, joined the Christ's College, Cambridge, passed the Natural Science Tripos of Cambridge University in 1884 and then gained a B.Sc. degree from London University. Among his teachers were renowned

J C Bose in his graduate gown in Cambridge.

scientists like Lord Rayleigh, Micheal Foster, Francis Darwin and Sidney Vines.

When Bose returned India in 1885, he joined the then Imperial Service of Education of the British Empire. He was appointed a Professor of Physics at the prestigious Presidency College, Kolkata. He was the first Indian to be appointed to this post.

In the nineteenth century, the British rulers treated Indians as an inferior race, with no inclination for science and experimentation. So naturally, even the most qualified Indian was not considered good enough to teach a difficult subject like physics.

When Bose was appointed as Professor of Physics in the Presidency College, it raised eyebrows everywhere in the British circles. Bose was offered a salary at two-thirds the scale of a British Professor's! And he was given half of the two-thirds amount because his post was temporary!

This unjust racial discrimination angered Bose. He had been brought up to respect equality, justice and brotherhood. He could not tolerate this and decided to lodge a protest. He therefore did not draw the salary, although he continued to teach his students with great enthusiasm and interest.

The Presidency College, Kolkata.

Those were trying days for the entire Bose family. He had meanwhile also got married to Abala. His father too had no means to help the young scientist. It became very difficult to manage even basic household expenses but Bose's father supported him fully in his fight against racial discrimination and injustice. He urged him to follow in the footsteps of Karna, one of the *Mahabharata* heroes, who always suffered defeats despite talent, abilities and sacrifices.

He taught Bose that success is always small and failure is great. in fact, he urged him to train his mind in such a way as to forget the difference between success and failure! His teachings were a source of inspiration for Bose at every step later in his life and came in handy during his years of arduous scientific research.

Once Bose also said, "If there has been any success in my life, that was built on the unshakable foundation of failure…"!

For the next three years, Bose continued to teach at the college without salary! He

Lady Abala Bose

19

ON A COMPLETE APPARATUS FOR THE STUDY OF THE PROPERTIES OF ELECTRIC WAVES.

By Jagadis Chunder Bose, M.A. (Cantab.), D.Sc. (Lond.),
Professor of Physical Science, Presidency College, Calcutta.

(Read before the British Association, 21st Sept., 1896.)

THE work of Hertz and his eminent successors, has opened out for study a new region of ethereal vibration, bridging over the gap that hitherto existed between the comparatively slow ether vibrations and the quick oscillations which give rise to radiant heat. In the vast range of possible ether vibrations we recognise only a few octaves by our senses; the rest are beyond our perception. Many unexpected properties of these little-known ether waves are now being gradually discovered. Confining our attention to the electric waves, we find that there are many important problems which may perhaps be better attacked with these comparatively slow vibrations; among which may be mentioned the determination of the indices of refraction of various substances which are opaque to visible light, but are transparent to the electric ray; the relation between the dielectric constant and the refractive index when the rates of oscillation are made comparable in the two determinations; the variation of the index with the frequencies of vibration. Then there are the phenomena of double refraction, polarisation, and the magnetic rotation of the electric ray; the determination of the wave-length, and other problems of a similar nature.

The fascination of the subject drew me to its study, though the investigations were rendered exceedingly difficult in India from want of facility for making the necessary apparatus. I ultimately succeeded in constructing a few instruments with which I was able to obtain the values of the indices of refraction of various substances for electric waves, the wave-length of electric radiation, and to demonstrate the phenomena of double refraction and polarisation of the electric rays. The simplified apparatus with which many of the properties of electromagnetic radiation may be studied is here exhibited. This is a duplicate was a popular teacher as students found his lectures interesting and attended them in large numbers. He also conducted research in a small, 24 square foot room allotted to him in the college.

Eventually, the British authorities could not keep their eyes closed to Bose's excellent skills at teaching. He was given the full salary right from the day he joined the college!

It was a big victory for Bose. It gave him courage and faith in his own fighting abilities, hard work and commitment. He also learnt that the best way to fight the British was to face them squarely with indomitable will.

CHAPTER THREE

Radio Waves Make Waves

Instant communication over the entire earth has today become possible due to radio waves, for messages, voices and pictures can be sent through them. Televisions. radios, cord-less phones, pagers, and mobile telephones are some common examples of gadgets that use radio waves for communication. At every moment radio waves are now being sent into space and are bouncing up and down over the earth. They have changed the lives of people completely, though their existence was demonstrated only more than a century ago, in 1864, by the British physicist James Clerk Maxwell. His mathematical equations showed that radio waves exist.

But nobody was ready to believe in the existence of radio waves until the German physicist Heinrich Hertz produced them in 1887. When a high voltage electric current was passed through a minute air gap between two terminals, an electric spark jumped across it completing the circuit and releasing radio waves. A lightning flash, which is essentially a huge electric spark, also produces radio waves. That is why disturbances called 'radio interferences' are observed in radio and television reception during thunderstorms and lightnings.

In due course, radio waves caught the imagination of several physicists in France, England, Russia and Italy. Their existence was demonstrated and properties studied.

(from the top): James Clerk Maxwell, Oliver Lodge and Heinrich Hertz.

23

Radio waves fascinated the British physicist Oliver Lodge who gave a lecture and then wrote a book *Heinrich Hertz and His Successors*. It was this book which created considerable interest in Europe and caught the attention of Bose who became interested in the subject of radio waves. The subject fascinated him so much that he began experiments on wireless telegraphy in the small space of 24 square feet allotted to him in the college laboratory. In fact, on his 35th birthday in 1894, he even took an oath to devote his life entirely to scientific research.

Using his own money, modifying devices and materials found after much search in scrap shops and taking the assistance of an illiterate tinsmith, Bose built the equipment necessary for the generation of radio waves. He designed and fabricated a novel type of 'radiator' for the generation of radio waves and also a unique and highly sensitive 'coherer' or radio receiver to catch them. His radio receiver consisting of spiral springs was far more compact, efficient and effective than those built in Europe in those days.

Using his equipment, Bose demonstrated various important properties of radio waves, like reflection and refraction. His experiments proved a fact that is well known today, that radio waves are similar to light. And it was then, that Bose made the important discovery that the speed of radio waves was equal to the speed of light—3 X 10^5 kilometres per second!

Moreover, Bose's equipment generated a novel type of radio waves— as small as 1 centimetre to 5 millimetre—now known as 'microwaves'. These radio waves are nowadays commonly used in radars, ground telecommunications, satellite communications, remote sensing and microwave ovens. His equipment was essentially the world's first wireless remote control. He had also invented then the world's first 'horn antenna', a conical-shaped antenna to catch microwaves, now commonly used in all microwave-related devices.

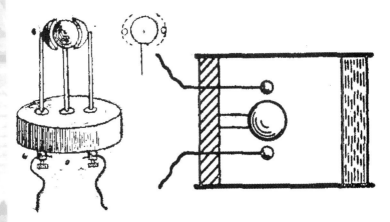

Bose's diagrams of his radiators 'spark gaps' which emit very short radio waves.

The successful demonstration of the generation and reception of radio waves to his students and colleagues created such a stir in the college that the authorities decided to stage its full-fledged demonstration before the Lieutenant Governor of Kolkata, Sir William Mackenzie.

This demonstration took place with pomp and show in the Town Hall of Kolkata in 1895 as narrated in the beginning of this book. The local newspapers hailed the successful demonstration of wireless telegraphy by an Indian inventor. It established Bose as one of the important successors of the German physicist Heinrich

Guglielmo Marconi in the wireless room of his yacht in 1920.

Guglielmo Marconi's apparatus of 1895.

Hertz in India. More than that, it has today established him as one of the pioneers of wireless telegraphy. It is also alleged that

Lord Rayleigh.

Guglielmo Marconi, who is today acclaimed as the inventor of the radio, had built his radio equipment borrowing ideas from Bose's work!

Subsequently, Bose intended to extend the range of his radio apparatus to about 1.6 kilometres so that radio signals could be transmitted from the Presidency College to his own residence. But he could not do so because he soon left for England on a lecture tour to demonstrate his findings before the British scientific community.

Earlier, Bose's findings on radio waves had been published in England. The University of London had bestowed upon him the Doctor of Science (D. Sc.) degree, and even as eminent a scientist as Lord Kelvin had congratulated him for his "wonderful experiments"! It was an exemplary achievement for an Indian who had no guidance in research and no proper laboratory facilities.

It was the twenty first of September, 1896.

The hall was crowded with scientists, technicians, technologists, science writers and science policy-makers. The occasion was a meeting of the British Association for the Advancement of Science at Liverpool, England. The hall was unusually crowded on that day, as the guest speaker was a curiosity for all Britishers. Even wives of some eminent scientists had come to attend the meeting and were sitting in the gallery overlooking the hall. For the first time in the history of the prestigious Association, an Indian scientist from Kolkata, Jagadish Chandra Bose, was to give a lecture-cum-demonstration on his novel findings on radio waves. There was an excitement in the air.

Bose himself was under tremendous tension since he had to address a gathering of eminent British men of science

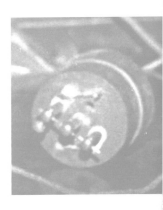

A close-up of the spark gaps normally mounted inside the transmitting antenna. The sparks between the gaps emit radio waves.

pertaining to a subject which he had explored on his own with indigenous equipment and without proper guidance. Not only was his own reputation at stake but also of his country because he was the first person to represent India in science before the western world. But when he stood up to speak, the words came so fluentty it was as though he had rehearsed them several times. Lantern

J.C. Bose at the Royal Institution, London, 1897.

slides and actual demonstrations of the properties of radio waves using his compact equipment further held the audience spellbound.

When Bose finished his speech and sat down, thundering applause greeted him. Even Lord Kelvin, the eminent scientist of the time, walked up leaning on a stick, climbed up to the gallery and congratulated Bose's wife Abala who was sitting over there. It was a moment of pride for all Indians. Jagadish Chandra Bose left an indelible mark in modern science which was till then considered to be the hunting ground of the western scientists.

Bose felt he had won his first battle on the western soil. True, it was his first victory but certainly not the last. Throughout his life, he continued to fight battles in science on the western soil because on several occasions his original and scientifically proven ideas were questioned and debated. Being the first and foremost Indian in the modern scientific world, his position was awkward, too. He was always waiting for an opportunity to prove to the western scientists that an Indian can also make an original contribution to science. "Everyone knows that we have brilliant imagination," he once said, "but I have to prove that we have accuracy and dogged persistence besides".

Subsequently, in the footsteps of great scientists like Michael Faraday

The apparatus of J. C. Bose which generated microwaves.

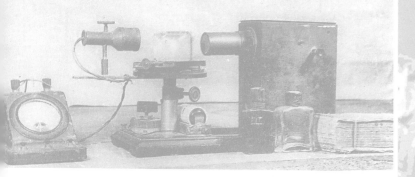

and Humphrey Davy, Bose also gave the Friday Evening Discourse at the prestigious Royal Institution in London, where more than five hundred scientists, including such luminaries like Oliver Lodge, J.J. Thomson and Lord Kelvin, were present. Not only was his lecture hailed but it was also considered valuable enough for publication in the prestigious scientific journal *Transactions of the Royal Institution.* Bose's lectures and demonstrations were considered special because it was only his novel equipment – and not those of his contemporary European inventors – that was capable of generating very minute radio waves 'microwaves' which were convenient to handle in a small space of a hall for demonstrations and experiments.

The news of the wonderful lectures and demonstrations of the Indian man of science spread to neighbouring France and Germany. He was then invited to give lecture-cum-demonstrations at various science bodies there also. Wherever he went in the West, he was praised and applauded.

The news of Bose's scientific successes in the West reached Indian shores quickly. Every Indian eagerly awaited his return. The Nobel Laureate Rabindranath Tagore was overjoyed at his feats. He even

A setup showing the transmitting antenna at the left, with the receiving antenna at right.

composed a poem in Bengali where he called Bose *Vijnan Laksmir Priya* – 'the Beloved of the Fairy of Science' and presented it to him as a blessing on his return to Kolkata in 1897.

Invigorated by his success. Bose took up his researches on radio waves with more enthusiasm and commitment. He continued to work in the same small laboratory space of the Presidency College. Surprisingly he had no complaints or regrets which would easily have troubled any other lesser mortal who had seen the best laboratories in the West.

In fact, some eminent British scientists, including Lord Lister, William Ramsey and Lord Kelvin, had in the meanwhile written to the then Indian Government to set up a research laboratory in the country so that Bose and other Indians could pursue research without any

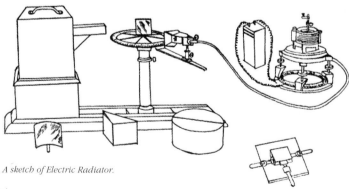

A sketch of Electric Radiator.

hindrances. Bose himself also began to think of setting up a laboratory in Kolkata where he could conduct his studies undisturbed. Thereafter, he and wife began to save every paisa for the dream laboratory.

In his studies of radio waves, Bose also modified the radio receiver so that it could catch not only radio waves but also visible and invisible light rays. He designed the whole equipment in the form of an eye and even called it an 'Electric eye'. For the purpose of detecting visible and invisible rays as well as radio waves, he selected a novel material, called 'galena', a compound of the metal lead. Today, galena, which has been found to be a 'semiconductor' with conductivity between that of a conductor and an insulator, is commonly used in all electronic equipment to catch radio waves as well as convert light rays into electricity. It has also laid the foundation of the subject of 'Optical communication' which uses light waves to exchange messages.

CHAPTER FOUR

From Metals to Plants

One day during an experiment, when Bose was ascertaining the electrical conductivity of his radio receiver, he observed a peculiar response. The receiver behaved normally when used intermittently. But when he used it continuously, its response became slow – as though it had become to 'tired' to respond! Bose was fascinated by this phenomenon which he called 'metal fatigue'. He therefore began to study in more detail this queer response that was not expected in metals. For this he used the highly sensitive current-detecting instrument called 'galvanometer'. A small mirror attached to the galvanometer pointer threw a spot of light on to a graduated scale, magnifying its response several times.

Slowly and gradually, Bose realised that perhaps metals too had feelings. To prove this theory, he designed a number of experiments because in science it is experiments that have the last word. He treated several metals, namely, tin, zinc, brass and platinum, with poisons, acids and heat, and studied their response. He found their behaviour changing with the treatment. For instance, it took considerable time for a metal to recover after treatment with poison or acid, its response also changed when it was slowly heated or slowly cooled!

It was then natural for Bose to shift his experiments on metals to plants because he was using considerable plant material like jute and paper during his experiments on radio waves. In fact, he found plants responding

One of the twisted-jute polarizers used by Bose.

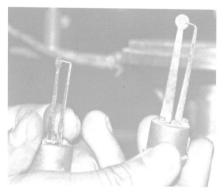

The galena detector of the 'Electric eye'.

more favourably to his experiments than metals.

Shortly, it dawned upon Bose that he had hit upon the underlying unity in the natural world between the inorganic, i.e., metals and the organic, i.e., plants. Bose was now exploring a new frontier in science. When he sent these findings to England for publication, it caused a stir in the European scientific community.

Everybody was keen to see Bose's experiments and demonstrations. Special arrangements were made for his travel so that he could participate in the most celebrated International Congress of Physics about to be held in Paris in 1900. He was also invited to the Paris Exhibition, where every year scientists, technologists and inventors from all over the world were invited to exhibit and demonstrate their novel findings and inventions before the scientific community and the public. It was a rare honour for any Indian scientist.

A photograph of Compound Lever Crescograph.

When Bose shifted from the study of radio waves to plants, he knew that he was entering the boundary of living and non-living, a totally new realm of science bordering both physics and biology but recognised by neither. Today, it is known as 'biophysics' and even comes under the latest frontiers of science, namely, 'cybernetics' and 'systems science. Working in his primitive laboratory, he was far ahead of his times. Morever, he did not know that while doing so he, as a physicist, was treading upon the feet of several reputed scientists studying the various processes occurring inside plants, who called themselves 'plant physiologists'!

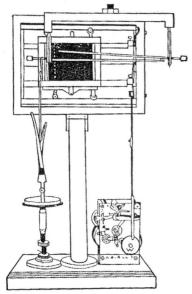

A sketch of Crescograph.

His experiments and demonstrations on metals and plants therefore evoked a mixed response from the European scientific community, whether it was Paris, London. Munich or Vienna. While physicists and chemists welcomed his new findings of the basic unity of all matter, plant physiologists were much more skeptical. Some well wishers even warned him to go step by step in a methodical and slow manner in this novel yet tricky subject lest he be treated as 'dreamy'.

However, wherever Bose went on lecture tours, the western press made a hero out of him for discovering the basic unity of life. It was felt that such a discovery could only be made by a scientist from the East, which has an age-old faith in this idea.

On May 10,1901, Bose faced his stiffest opposition, when he gave the famous Friday Evening Discourse at the Royal Institution, London. Two eminent British plant physiologists, John Burd on-Sanderson and Augustus Waller, stood up after his lecture and, after praising some features of the experiments, strongly criticized him for using a word like 'response' for metals and plants which they felt was strictly reserved for living beings. They instead suggested the use of the words 'chemical reaction'. Then they went on to ensure that his lecture and subsequent research papers did not find a place in the reputed publications of the Royal Institution as well as the Royal Society!

Bose was rather put off by the ban, as it was based merely on his using certain words and terms in his lecture and research papers.

He felt the whole matter was being handled in an unscientific manner! But opposition and criticism were not new to him. He prepared himself to fight tooth and nail for the truth that he had discovered. He knew that any new idea was always difficult to digest and initially faces stiff opposition. So he decided to conduct more rigorous experiments in England to prove his theory and did not wait for his return to the laboratory at home.

Bose conducted experiments in the reputed Davy-Faraday Laboratory of the Royal Institution, where far more sophisticated equipment and facilities were available. Later, when he found that

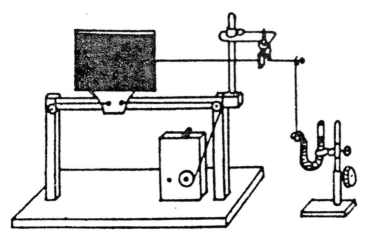

Bose's Plant Photograph.

his own experiments were published under their demonstration in the public someone else's name, then he realised that he must publish his findings before their in the public demonstration. In fact, he decided to publish his findings in the form of books devoted entirely to specialised subjects called 'monographs'. During his life time, he wrote 10 monographs on plant physiology. However, the one which brought him fame was the controversial monograph

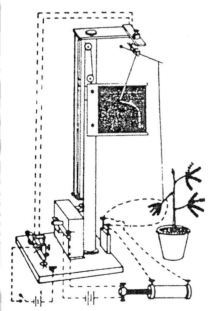

– *Response in the Living and the Non-Living*, which was published in England in 1902.

Although Bose continued his experiments in Europe for the next two years, the time to return home arrived soon. His British hosts therefore offered him a research-cum-teaching job at a prestigious British university so that he could continue his experiments there.

Bose's Resonant Recorder.

A lesser mortal would have easily agreed but not Bose. The call of the motherland was too strong for him. He returned home with the strong commitment to prove his theory working in an Indian environment. Moreover, being an Indian, he also knew the honour of his country was at stake. It was to be restored at all cost.

It was also during his long stay in Europe that one British businessman, Dr Alexender Muirhead approached Bose with a patent form before his controversial lecture at the Royal Institution in 1901. He suggested that Bose should not reveal too much about his radio receiver during the lecture because he intended to patent it on his behalf. He offered Bose half the money that would accrue from its sales because by then wireless telegraphy was gaining popularity in Europe and America. It was being used to receive messages from ships at sea or in fog.

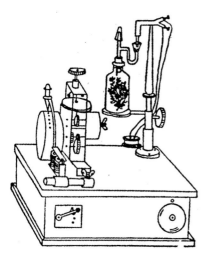

Bose's Photosynthetic Recorder.

But Bose was then in no mood to listen to any such commercial gain out of his invention, as he was committed to the search for truth. He felt that money would corrupt his mind and lead him astray from his real aspirations in life.

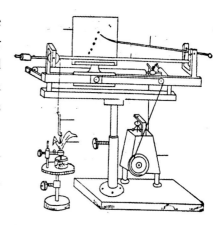

A sketch of Compound Lever Crescograph.

Frankly speaking, Bose actually lost a golden opportunity. Had he gone in for a patent for his highly efficient radio receiver, he would have not only received considerable money needed to build his dream laboratory in India. He could also have received world recognition and immortality in the annuals of wireless telegraphy and radio.

45

CHAPTER FIVE

Creation of the Bose Institute

Bose's discovery of the basic unity of life had meanwhile caught the attention of several renowned philosophers and writers. Eminent persons like Romain Rolland, George Bernard Shaw, Vivekananda and Rabindra Nath Tagore were his great admirers. They all felt that he had given a fresh, scientific impetus to the age-old wisdom of the East which believed in the basic unity of all life. A British Editor once wrote, "In Sir Jagadish the culture of thirty centuries has blossomed into a scientific brain of an order which we cannot duplicate in the West"!

In fact, after his famous lecture on the similarities between the living and the non-living when Bose travelled in Europe, America and Japan, this discovery rather than his work on radio waves was publicised more in reputed newspapers and magazines. That was natural as the subject was more interesting and easier to understand. Several cartoons on Bose as well as his discovery also appeared in the press. For instance, after a lecture in Paris, a leading French newspaper wrote "After this discovery we begin to have misgivings, when we strike a woman with a blossom, which of them suffers more – the woman or the flower"! In fact, he became one of the most talked about scientists in the world of the early 1900s.

Naturally, such accolades would boost the morale, commitment and enthusiasm of

J C Bose with Rabindra Nath Tagore; Vivekananda and Romain Rolland were also among his great admirers.

47

any scientist. Bose was therefore carried away emotionally by his novel discovery. He devoted himself fully to laying his new yet controversial discovery on the firm foundation of a theory at the cost of his very important work in radio waves. He thereafter put all his resources, assistants and facilities at the Presidency College and then at the newly established Bose Institute to the systematic and detailed studies of plants.

In those days, all the phenomena seen in plants, such as, growth, death, reaction to forces or chemicals, were explained in terms of the movement and pressure of sap occurring in its roots, stem, branches and leaves. It was Bose who through his classic experiments showed that very minute pulses of electricity coursing through different parts of plants explained several of these phenomena.

To conduct these studies Bose invented several novel and highly sensitive instruments to measure the electrical pulses for understanding the phenomena. The most famous of these instruments is the 'Crescograph' for measuring the rate of growth of a plant. It could record a growth as small as 1/100,000 inch per second! Another famous invention is the 'Death-recorder' for recording the precise moment when a plant dies. Initially, he gave interesting Sanskrit names to the instruments. For instance, the Death-recorder was called 'Morograph' because 'moro' means 'death' in Sanskrit. But, later, he gave up the practice when he found that western scientists had a problem pronouncing the names. Today one can still see some of these instruments in working conditions in the J.C. Bose Museum of the Bose Institute in Kolkata.

Most of Bose's experiments were performed on two well known plants, viz; *Mimosa pudica* and *Desmondium gyrans*. The former is considered to be an extremely sensitive plant as it droops its leaves as soon as it is touched. The latter pulsates as though it contains an animal heart.

Bose showed that all plants behave like human beings. They have 'nerves' through which they can sense pleasure and pain. When they are wounded or treated with heat, cold or electric shock, they take considerable time to recover and their reaction time changes. They die when they are poisoned. They fall unconscious when treated with an anaesthetic. They behave

Mimosa pudica *and* Desmondium gyrans.

49

groggily when they are given a dose of alcohol! Bose also measured the rate of growth of plants during various stages of their life and tried to ascertain the reasons behind their behaviour on basis of his electrical studies. His findings subsequently influenced subjects like physiology, medicine and agriculture.

Unlike most Indian scientists, Bose also tried to explore the scientific reasons behind some Indian superstitions associated with plants and trees. For instance, he found that the change in temperature of the surroundings responsible for the behaviour of the very sacred and popular 'Praying Palm' in Faridpur. The date palm was believed to droop its branches as though bowing to the neighbouring God when temple bells were rung in the evening and raised them again in the morning when they were rung.

"This temple is dedicated to the feet of God for bringing honour to India and happiness to the world," said Bose, when the Bose Institute was formally opened for research on November 30, 1917. While Tagore's song composed for the opening ceremony was sung, messages of congratulations and best wishes for the institute were received from all over the world, including China.

Throughout his life, Bose had felt the handicap of a good laboratory with sophisticated equipment and facilities where Indian scientists

The Bose Institute, Kolkata.

could pursue their research interests undisturbed and unhindered. Moreover, he was keen to set up a seat of learning in the tradition of ancient Indian universities of Nalanda and once Taxila, which attracted scholars from all parts of the world. So, when he retired

J.C. Bose and Lady Bose with the staff members of The Bose Institute.

from the college with the honorary title of 'Emeritus Scientist' presented by the then Government, he concentrated on fulfilling his age-old dream of setting up a laboratory devoted to plant studies.

Over the years Bose himself had saved a considerable amount of money for this purpose. Tagore further helped him by introducing him to several Princes of Indian states, political leaders and philanthropists from all over India, who gave donations and yearly grants for the laboratory. The Maharaja of Tripura particularly gave a handsome donation for the laboratory. Bose even went on a fund-raising campaign to different parts of the country.

Eventually, in 1917, on his 59th birthday, the foundation of what is today known as the 'Bose Institute' was laid on a four acre plot on what is now known as Acharya Prafulla Chandra Road in Kolkata. Surrounded with gardens, the institute was designed in the Mauryan style. Apart from laboratories the institute also had a workshop, a library and lecture halls. A regular publication called *Transactions of the Bose Institute* to record the work done at the institute was also subsequently brought out. The institute also offered scholarships and fellowships for Indian or foreign scholars for research and training there.

Here in the laboratories of the institute, Bose devoted the rest of his life solely to the study of plants. He worked till he breathed his last on November 23, 1937 at Giridih, a hill station near Kolkata,, where he went for a short vacation. His ashes were interred in the compound of the institute.

Bose was not an ivory tower scientist in the sense he was devoted to his research only. He was an orator, who could present his technical findings in an understandable manner to the public. In fact, he took considerable pains to make his findings accessible to the public by using illustrations and slide shows. To popularise his discoveries he even wrote about his findings in Bengali magazines.

Bose's ability at communication led to lavish praise of him as a scientist and his wonderful findings on plants were always highlighted in the newspapers of the western countries where he lectured.

A great lover of music, Bose also wrote poetry and short stories. In fact, once he was also elected as the President of the state level literary body, Bangiya Sahitya Parishad. At a literary meet of the Parishad at Mymensingh, he gave an address on 'Literature in Science'. He was fond of travelling and twice in a year he and his wife would visit places of historical importance, pilgrimages and scenic beauty. He was especially fond of visiting the banks of large rivers.

Bose was admired as a 'Scientist-hero' during his life-time because he was the pioneer of modern Indian science. Apart from several British Government's honours and knighthood, he was also elected a Fellow of the Royal Society in 1920. However, very little is known about his scientific crusade and achievements today. Even his revolutionary field of research on plants, called 'Plant Electrophysiology', did not catch on in the country! There are several reasons behind this tragedy.

First, Bose did not patent his invention which would have made his position secure and clear in the field of radio waves. Quite likely, he would have even shared the Nobel Prize with Guglielmo Marconi had he done so. Secondly, he gave up the new field of microwaves which he himself had discovered and which received importance only after his death. Had he continued his researches on microwaves his rating as a physicist would certainly have been higher today when the usage of these waves is common. Thirdly, he did not train a group of young scientists who could follow in his footsteps in plant electro-physiology. Last but not the least, though good to his students throughout 35 years of teachership, he conducted research alone and often single-handedly.

Sayings of J C Bose

Is there anything you cannot do if you put
your whole mind to it?

■

Learn once for all to choose what you are going to do,
and say I will.

■

There can be no happiness for any of us unless
it has been won for all.

■

As a candle can only be lighted by another burning candle,
a true teacher alone can ignite enthusiasm in his disciples.

CHRONOLOGY

Headlines of J C Bose

1858 Born at Mymensingh in Dacca district, now in Bangladesh.

1869 Admitted to the Hare School, Kolkata.

1878 Passed B.A. from St. Xavier's College, Kolkata.

1880 Left India for the U.K. for higher studies.

1884 Passed B.A. in science from Cambridge University, U.K.

1885 Appointed Professor of Physics in Presidency College, Kolkata.

1894 Invented the wireless telegraphy equipment.

1895 Demonstrated the radio equipment at Town Hall of Kolkata.

1896 Visited the U.K., France and Germany for the demonstration of the wireless equipment. Returned the next year.

1900 Attended the International Congress of Physics held in Paris. Presented the controversial paper 'On the Similarity of Responses in Inorganic and Living Matter' in Paris and London, and elsewhere.

1903 Honoured with C.I.E. (Commander of the Order of the Indian Empire) at Delhi Durbar by the British Government.

1912 Received C.S.I. (Commander of the Star of India) at the Coronation of the British Emperor.

1915 Retired from Presidency College. Appointed 'Emeritus Professor' for life by the British Government.

1916 Received Knighthood of the British Government.

1917 Founded the Bose Institute at Kolkata.

1920 Elected a Fellow of the Royal Society, London.

1937 Died at Giridih, near Kolkata.

BIBLIOGRAPHY

Anonymous, Indian Scientists: Biographical Sketches,
G.A.Natesan & Co Publishers, 1925

Gupta, Monoranjon, Jagadish Chandra Bose -a biography,
Bharatiya Vidya Bhawan, 1964

Singh, Jagjit, Some Eminent Indian Scientists,
Publications Division, 1966

Basu, S.N., Jagadish Chandra Bose,
National Book Trust, 1970

Nandy, Ashis, Alternative Sciences-Creativity and Authenticity in Two Indian
Scientists, Allied Publishers Pvt Ltd, 1980

Dasgupta, Subrata, Jagadish Chandra Bose - and the Indian Response to Western
Science, Oxford University Press, 1999

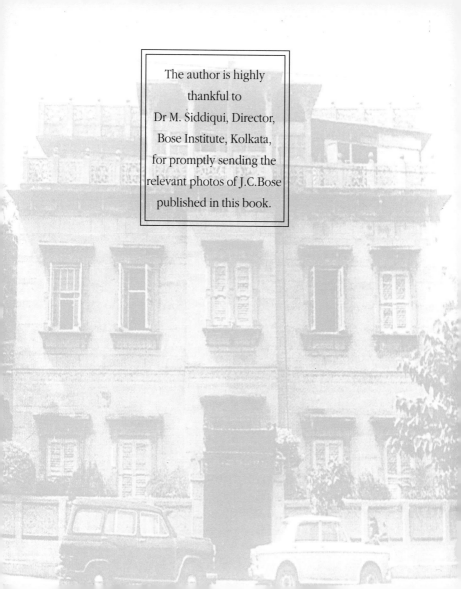

The author is highly
thankful to
Dr M. Siddiqui, Director,
Bose Institute, Kolkata,
for promptly sending the
relevant photos of J.C.Bose
published in this book.

NOTES